Study the alphabet and number chart.

Manuscript Writing

Look at the arrows. Trace the numbers.
Now write the numbers.

1   2   3   4   5

6   7   8   9   0

Manuscript Writing

Look at the arrows. Trace each letter.
Now write the letters and words.

A A

a a

Annie

ant

Look at the arrows. Trace each letter.
Now write the letters and words.

B B

b b

Billy

bear

Look at the arrows. Trace each letter.
Now write the letters and words.

C C

c c

Casey

cat

Look at the arrows. Trace each letter.
Now write the letters and words.

D D D

d d d

David

duck

6

Look at the arrows. Trace each letter.
Now write the letters and words.

E E

e e

Ellie

elf

Look at the arrows. Trace each letter.
Now write the letters and words.

F F

f f

Fran

fox

Look at the arrows. Trace each letter.
Now write the letters and words.

G G

g g

Gary

goat

Look at the arrows. Trace each letter.
Now write the letters and words.

H H

h h

Harry

horse

Look at the arrows. Trace each letter.
Now write the letters and words.

I I

i i

Ike

iguana

Look at the arrows. Trace each letter.
Now write the letters and words.

J J

j j

Jason

jay

Look at the arrows. Trace each letter.
Now write the letters and words.

K K

k k

Kelly

koala

Look at the arrows. Trace each letter.
Now write the letters and words.

L L

l l

Leah

lion

Look at the arrows. Trace each letter.
Now write the letters and words.

m m

Mandy

mouse

15

Manuscript Writing

Look at the arrows. Trace each letter.
Now write the letters and words.

Nn

n n

Nina

newt

Look at the arrows. Trace each letter.
Now write the letters and words.

O O

o o

Omar

owl

Look at the arrows. Trace each letter.
Now write the letters and words.

 P

 p

Peter

panda

Look at the arrows. Trace each letter.
Now write the letters and words.

Q Q Q

q q q

Quincy

quail

Look at the arrows. Trace each letter.
Now write the letters and words.

 R R

 r r

Rich

rabbit

Look at the arrows. Trace each letter.
Now write the letters and words.

S S

s s

Sally

seal

Look at the arrows. Trace each letter.
Now write the letters and words.

T T

t t

Tony

turtle

Look at the arrows. Trace each letter.
Now write the letters and words.

U U

u u

Ursula

unicorn

Look at the arrows. Trace each letter.
Now write the letters and words.

V v

V v

Vicky

vulture

Look at the arrows. Trace each letter.
Now write the letters and words.

Wendy

wolf

Look at the arrows. Trace each letter.
Now write the letters and words.

X X X

x x x

Xavier

x-ray

Look at the arrows. Trace each letter.
Now write the letters and words.

Y Y

y y

Yancy

yak

Look at the arrows. Trace each letter.
Now write the letters and words.

Z Z

z z

Zack

zebra

Practice writing your name.

Wasn't that fun?

Practice writing your address and phone number.

My name
is
Randy.